TITLE	PAGE

70s

January 21, 1976... the midday crowd gathered at Heathrow looked on excitedly as a British Airways jet roared into the sky bound for Bahrain.

At precisely the same time, an identical aircraft bearing the banner of Air France left Roissy-Charles-de-Gaulle airport in Paris with 83 passengers on board, headed to Rio via Dakar.

No ordinary jets, these were the new Concordes, and on that winter's day in the middle of the 1970s, they would make history as the first passenger planes to travel faster than the speed of sound. Taking off into the January sky, the two supersonic jets represented more than a milestone in aviation; they heralded a new spirit of European unity and co-operation.

The Concordes were the products of an unusual treaty, an agreement that would have been unimaginable in an earlier time, a pact between the British and French governments to work jointly on the development of a supersonic jet liner. As they soared above the clouds over London and Paris, the two majestic aircraft offered gleaming proof that a new, more unified era had dawned in Europe.

This was part of an enduring legacy that the '70s would leave to European history. The European Union, Airbus, the Euro, and so many of the other features of our contemporary "untied" Europe trace their origins, either directly or indirectly, to events that unfolded in these often-misunderstood years.

The '70s was the first decade of the post-colonial era. For the first time in centuries, the nations of Europe, with few exceptions, had no overseas colonies. This decade also marked the start of the post-industrial era. Many of the

PIANO/VOCAL/CHORDS

100 YEARS OF POPULAR MUSIC

70s - Volume 1

Series Editor:
Carol Cuellar

Editorial and Production:
Artemis Music Limited

Design and Production:
JPCreativeGroup.com

Published 2003

International Music Publications Limited
Griffin House 161 Hammersmith Road London W6 8BS England

IMP
International MUSIC Publications

CONTENTS

FIGHT II...THE BIG FIGHT EVERYONE IS WAITING TO SEE
MADISON SQ. GARDEN | MON. JAN. 28th

MAIN EVENT — 12 ROUNDS
JOE
FRAZIER
PHILA — FORMER WORLD HEAVYWEIGHT CHAMPION
1964 OLYMPIC CHAMPION
vs.
MUHAMMAD
ALI
LOUISVILLE KY. — FORMER WORLD HEAVYWEIGHT CHAMPION
1960 OLYMPIC CHAMPION
OTHER GREAT HEAVYWEIGHT FIGHTS
PRICES $100 RINGSIDE AND LOGE $75 $50 $40 $30 $20 MEZZANINE

the '70s. It was in this decade that the first true "Euro sound" emerged in rock and roll. Earlier European artists, particularly the Merseybeat groups of the '60s, had reached the top of the rock charts and inspired legions of imitators in other countries, including the US. But the underlying sound of European rock had always been derived from American roots – until the '70s.

In this decade, a distinct European rock sound had emerged, complete with its own techno mixes, rhythmic inflections, and unique musical flavour. With its clippy dance beat, lush vocals, and richly textured instrumentation, the new European music was clearly different from its American counterpart.

stable "smoke-stack" industries that had been the primary measure of a nation's economic might since the 19th Century seemed to sink beneath their own weight in the '70s. In their place emerged new, more nimble high-tech fields that were driven by computers and electronics, rather than coal and steel.

Faced with new challenges and rapidly changing times, the nations of Europe turned toward one another for help, pooling their resources, talents, and markets in new co-operative ventures. In 1973, the United Kingdom was admitted to the European Economic Community (EEC). By the end of the decade, the European Monetary System was established, and the continent was well on the way toward achieving the unity that plays such an important role in our society today.

This difference is very evident in songs like "Baker Street" by Scottish-born Gerry Rafferty, which just missed being No.1 in the UK in 1978. Rafferty's smash hit, with its haunting lyrics backed by subtle bass and keyboard, featured a lush and evocative saxophone introduction by session player Raphael Ravenscroft. The unforgettable sax line by Ravenscroft became instantly recognisable to music fans everywhere, including America, where the *City To City* album that featured "Baker Street" reached the top of the charts.

The Euro Sound

This new European spirit was also evident in the music of

Indeed, many popular American artists of the '70s began incorporating the Euro sound into their own repertoires. Barry Manilow was clearly

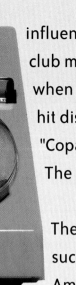

influenced by the Euro club music of the '70s, when he recorded his hit disco tune "Copacabana (At The Copa)".

The immensely successful American group Blondie also drew heavily on Europe for inspiration. Formed in New York in 1974 after Deborah Harry and Fred Smith left the Stilettos, Blondie grew out of the city's underground punk scene. The group's distinctive sound, which combined playful but edgy lyrics with a driving melody, was often too forward for the American market during its early days, but it was readily accepted in England.

Always ready to incorporate new influences, Blondie welcomed British bassist Nigel Harrison into the group. British producer/songwriter Mike Chapman and German disco producer Giorgio Moroder also worked closely with Blondie at different times during the '70s, giving the group's music an even more pronounced European flavour.

By the end of the '70s, Blondie was enjoying spectacular success throughout Europe and America. The group closed out the decade with a cover of John Holt's song "The Tide Is High". This reggae inspired tune reached No.1 on the UK and US charts. It was the fifth chart-topping

hit for Blondie in Britain during an incredible two-year span.

The popularity of the *Eurovision Song Contest* television programme contributed to the growth of the European sound during the '70s. Sponsored by the state-run European TV stations, this show attracted large audiences and helped launch the careers of many aspiring European musicians. In 1970, the contest was won by Dana Rosemary Scallon, the first Irish artist to achieve this honour, for the beautiful "All Kinds Of Everything". Other would-be stars who entered the contest were less fortunate than Scallon. In 1973, a young quartet named Bjorn, Benny, Agnetha and Frida entered, but finished third in the qualifying round in their native Sweden. Undaunted, the foursome returned the next year with new material and became the first Swedish artists to win the prestigious event.

Building on their first place finish, the group went on to become one of the most popular groups of the '70s or any decade under their new name, ABBA. Attractive and dynamic with a musical style that managed to be fun,

romantic, sophisticated, and carefree all at once, ABBA achieved world-wide success on a level that was nothing short of phenomenal. During one three-year period, the group had thirteen Top Five hits in the UK, a half dozen of which reached the top of the charts.

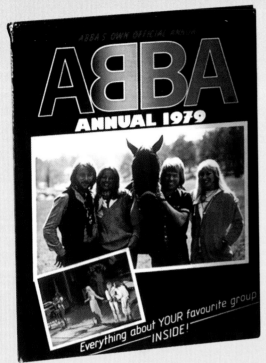

ABBA songs like the catchy "Chiquitita". still receive a great deal of air play today. Although ABBA broke up in 1982, its recordings continue to sell in the millions around the world. In 1995 the group's popularity received a further boost, when its songs were featured in the hit Australian film *Muriel's Wedding*.

From Folk To Films

Pop music not only became more international in the '70s, it also embraced a wider variety of genres. In Britain, America, and elsewhere, folk music came out of the rural pubs and city coffee-houses to reach mainstream fans and influence the direction of pop music.

Ralph McTell's simple, but evocative, folk song "Streets Of London" became one of the biggest international hits of the mid-70s, reaching No.2 on the UK charts. At one point, the German charts included four different versions of this heartfelt ballad. Born Ralph May in Kent, the future British folk star began playing harmonica at seven, later learning the ukulele to play in a skiffle band and, from there, migrated to the guitar. By the 1960s, McTell had attracted a large following playing in the clubs of Soho. By the 1970s, the growing popularity of folk music allowed him to achieve more mainstream success. In 1974, the same year his recording of "Streets Of London" became an international hit, McTell became the first solo act to sell out The Royal Albert Hall in 14 years.

Interestingly, "Streets Of London" was only the third song that this talented artist ever wrote. In the years since McTell penned this tune, it has been recorded over 200 times by performers as diverse as Bruce Springsteen and Aretha Franklin.

Like the folk songs of Ralph McTell, the music of film and stage also touched people around the world in the '70s, the decade when mass media took major strides to becoming truly international. In 1975, the American superstar Diana Ross had a cross-cultural hit with "Do You Know Where You're Going To", the theme song from her film *Mahogany*.

The great Welsh singer Shirley Bassey had a hit on both sides of the Atlantic in

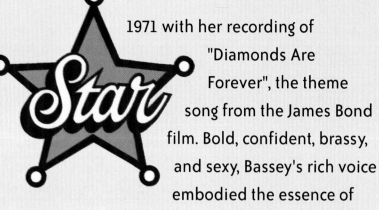

1971 with her recording of "Diamonds Are Forever", the theme song from the James Bond film. Bold, confident, brassy, and sexy, Bassey's rich voice embodied the essence of the James Bond mystique. It's no wonder that she recorded three of the most popular songs in the history of this famous film franchise.

Although Bassey won a large international fan following, her warmth and passionate vocal style earned a special place in the hearts of British music lovers. In 1977, she won the Britannia Award for "Best Female Solo Singer of the Last 50 Years".

From the world of theatre, one of the biggest international hits was Judy Collins' 1975 recording of "Send In The Clowns". This haunting, bittersweet song was taken from Broadway composer Stephen Sondheim's production *A Little Night Music*, itself inspired by the Ingmar Bergman film *Smiles Of A Summer Night*. So here is a song recorded by a folk singer from a New York composer's production that grew out of a Swedish movie... As we noted, the '70s were indeed a time when popular music welcomed the whole world.

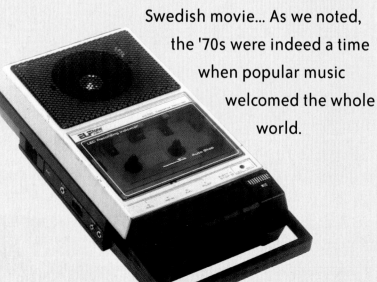

Ten Things That First Appeared In The '70s

1. **Designer jeans.**
2. **Personal computers.**
3. **Child-proof bottles.**
4. **Word processors.**
5. **Floppy disks.**
6. **Disposable razors.**
7. **VCR (video cassette recorder).**
8. **Artificial heart.**
9. **Laser printers.**
10. **Test-tube babies.**

ALL KINDS OF EVERYTHING

Words and Music by DERRY LINDSAY and JACK SMITH

AMARILLO (IS THIS THE WAY TO)

Words and Music by NEIL SEDAKA and HOWARD GREENFIELD

Is this the way to Am - a- ril - lo, ev-'ry night I've been hug - ging my pil - low,

dream -ing dreams of Am - a- ril - lo, and sweet Ma-rie who waits__ for me.

Show me the way to Am - a- ril - lo, I've been weep-in' like__ a wil - low,

Cry-ing ov-er Am - a-ril-lo and sweet Ma-rie who waits___ for me.

Sha la-la la la___ la la la   Sha-la-la la la___ la la la   Sha-la-la la la___

1.

2.

D. S. and repeat till fade

___ la la la   And Ma-rie who waits___ for me.   for me.

D. S. and repeat till fade

AND I LOVE YOU SO

Words and Music by DON McLEAN

BEAUTIFUL SUNDAY

Words and Music by DANIEL BOONE and ROD McQUEEN

Sun - day morn - ing, up with the lark, I think I'll take a walk in the park.
Birds are sing - ing, you by my side, let's take a car and go for a ride.

Hey hey hey, it's a beau - ti - ful day!
Hey hey hey, it's a beau - ti - ful day!

I've got some-one wait-ing for me,— and when I see her I know that she'll say,—
We'll drive on— and fol-low the sun,— mak-in' Sun-day go on and on.—

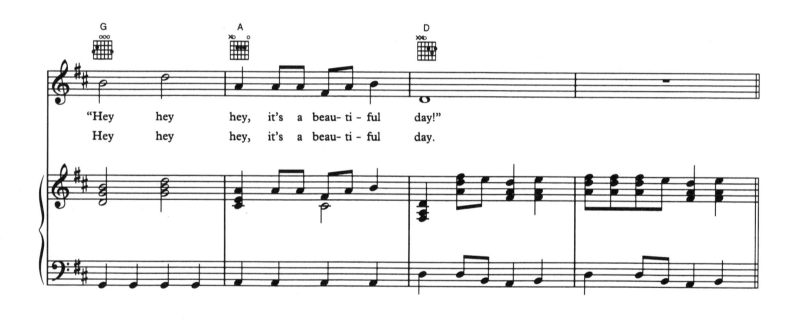

"Hey hey hey, it's a beau-ti-ful day!"
Hey hey hey, it's a beau-ti-ful day.

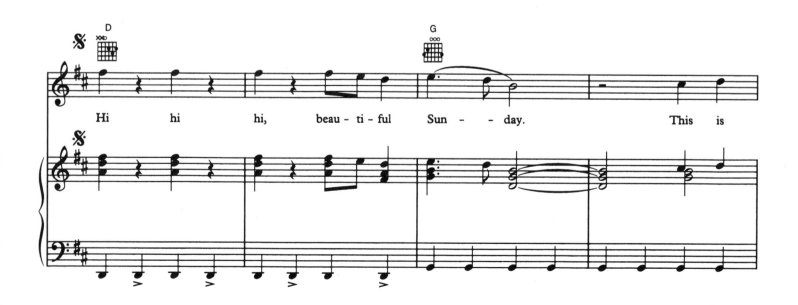

Hi hi hi, beau-ti-ful Sun-day. This is

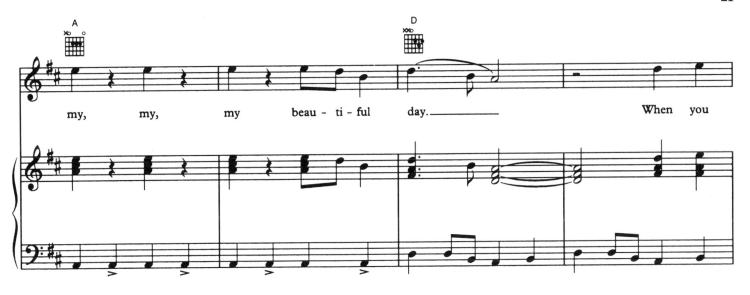

my, my, my beau-ti-ful day.———— When you

said, said, said, said that you loved——— me, oh,————

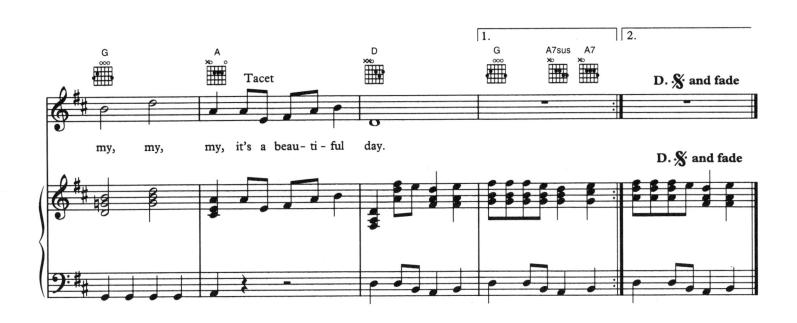

my, my, my, it's a beau-ti-ful day.

Tacet

1. 2.

D. 𝄋 and fade

D. 𝄋 and fade

CAN YOU READ MY MIND

Words by LESLIE BRICUSSE
Music by JOHN WILLIAMS

CHANSON D'AMOUR

Words and Music by WAYNE SHANKLIN

ra da da da da chan - son,___ chan - son___ d'a - mour.

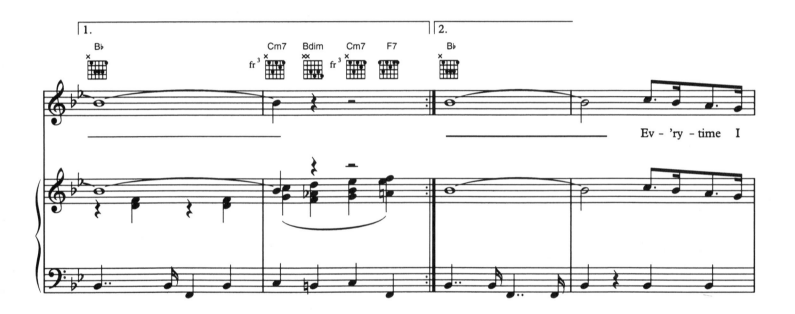

Ev - 'ry - time I

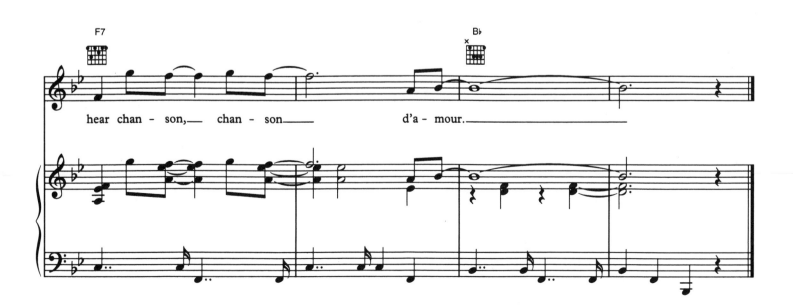

hear chan - son,___ chan - son___ d'a - mour.___

DAUGHTER OF DARKNESS

Words and Music by LES REED and GEOFF STEPHENS

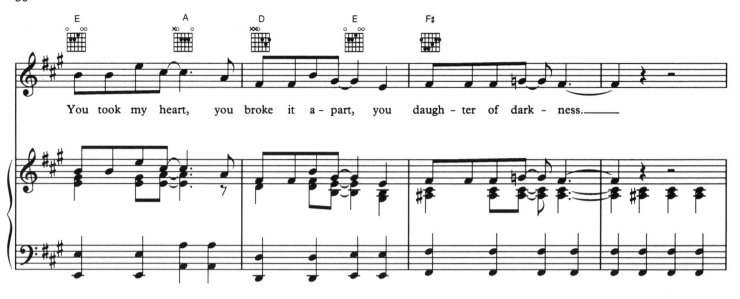

You took my heart, you broke it a - part, you daugh - ter of dark - ness.____

Daugh - ter of dark - ness leave me a - lone for ev - er, daugh - ter of dark - ness,

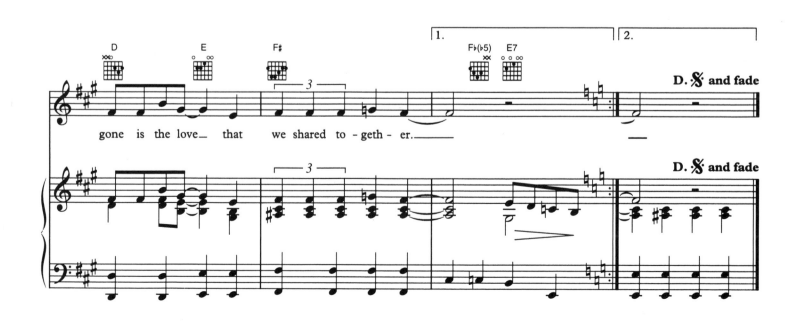

gone is the love__ that we shared to - geth - er.____

D. %. and fade

D. %. and fade

DAY BY DAY

Words and Music by STEPHEN SCHWARTZ

fol - low Thee more near - ly,___ day by___ day.___

day by day.___ Day by day,___

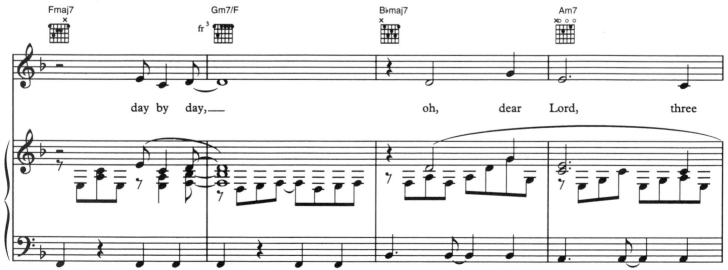

day by day,___ oh, dear Lord, three

DAY TRIP TO BANGOR
(DIDN'T WE HAVE A LOVELY TIME)

Words and Music by DEBBIE COOK

DON'T GIVE UP ON US

Words and Music by TONY MACAULAY

DIAMONDS ARE FOREVER

Words by DON BLACK
Music by JOHN BARRY

Dia-monds are for-ev-er,_____ they are all I need to please me,_____ they can stim-u-late and tease me,_____ they won't leave in the night, I've no fear that they might de-

sert me._____ Dia -monds are for-ev- er,_____ hold one
Dia -monds are for-ev- er,_____ spark -ling

up and then ca -ress it,_____ touch it, stroke it and un -dress it,_____
round my lit -tle fin -ger._____ Un -like men, the dia -monds lin -ger;_____

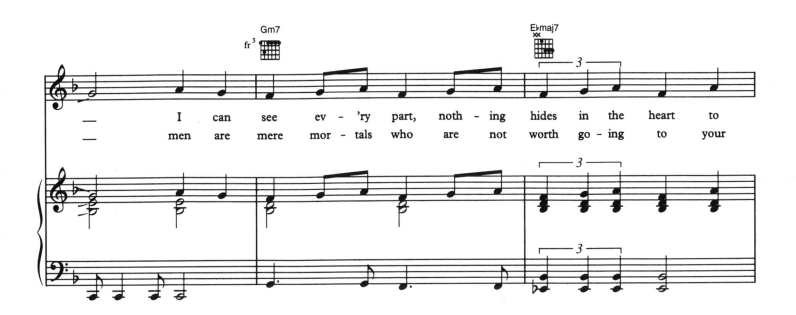

__ I can see ev -'ry part, noth -ing hides in the heart to
__ men are mere mor -tals who are not worth go -ing to your

DO YOU KNOW WHERE YOU'RE GOING TO?

Words by GERRY GOFFIN
Music by MICHAEL MASSER

DON'T CRY OUT LOUD

Words and Music by CAROLE BAYER SAGER and PETER ALLEN

1. Ba - by cried the day the cir - cus came to town, 'cause she
2. Ba - by saw the day they pulled the big top down, they

did - n't like pa - rades just pass - ing by her. So she
left be - hind her dreams a - mong the lit - ter.

paint - ed on a smile and took up with some clown, and she
And the dif - f'rent kind of love she thought she'd found, was

DON'T IT MAKE MY BROWN EYES BLUE

Words and Music by RICHARD LEIGH

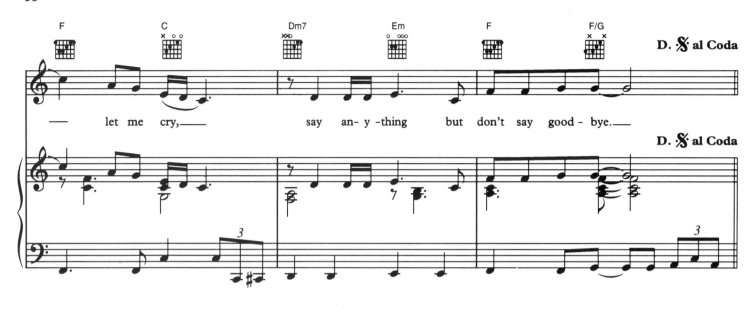

D. %̱ al Coda

— let me cry,—— say an-y-thing but don't say good-bye.——

D. %̱ al Coda

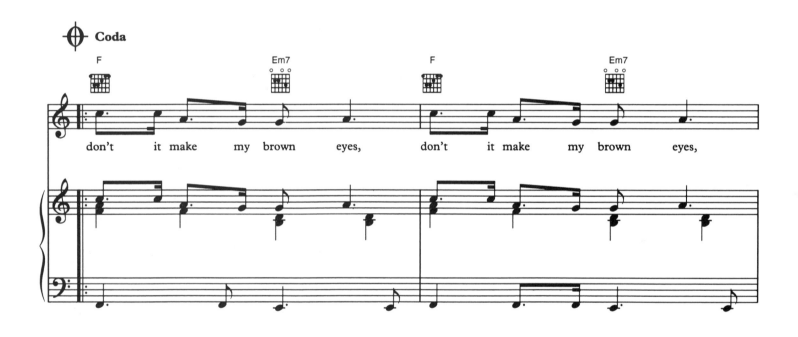

Coda

don't it make my brown eyes, don't it make my brown eyes,

repeat and fade

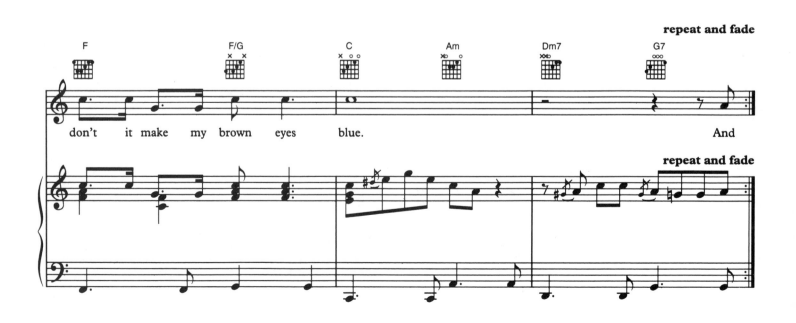

don't it make my brown eyes blue. And

repeat and fade

DON'T STAY AWAY TOO LONG

Original Words by GEORG BUSCHOR
English Words by BRYAN ANDRE BLACKBURN
Music by HENRY MAYER

It's time that you were go – ing and there's no way of know – ing
I'll miss you ev – 'ry min – ute my world with – out you in it.

how long we'll be a – part. Wher – ev – er life may lead you. Re –
Is such an emp – ty place. When days bring rain – y wea – ther, as

mem – ber how I need you, keep our love locked in your heart! Oh, oh,
long as we're to – geth – er there is no – thing we can't face.

jet plane fly – in' high a – bove me. Don't stay a – way too

long. Come back dar – lin', say you love me.

EVERYTHING IS BEAUTIFUL

Words and Music by RAY STEVENS

There is none so blind_____ as he who will not see._____
We should – n't care 'bout the length of his hair or the co – lour of his skin._____

We must not close our minds,_____ we must let our thoughts be
Don't wor – ry a – bout what shows from with – out, but the love that lives with–

free._____ For ev – 'ry hour that pas – ses by_____
in._____ We gon – na get it all to – geth – er now

FEELINGS

English Words and Music by MORRIS ALBERT
Spanish Words by THOMAS FUNDORA and LOUIS GASTE

you'll nev - er come a - gain.
Ja - más tu vol - ve - rás.

D. %. al Coda

⊕ *Coda*

Feel - ings,
¿Di - me?

wo wo wo,
Wo wo wo

feel - ings,
¿Di - me?

wo wo wo,
Wo wo wo

feel - ings
¿Di - me?

Repeat and fade

a - gain in my arms.
A - quí en mas bra - zos.

mp

f

THE FIRST TIME EVER I SAW YOUR FACE

Words and Music by EWAN MacCOLL

and the moon_____ and the stars_____   were the
like the trem - -bling heart_____   of a
and I knew our joy_____   would_____

3rd time to coda

gifts you gave_____   to_____ the dark____
cap - - -tive bird_____   that____ was there____
fill the earth____

3rd time to coda

3rd time D. C. al coda

and the emp - -ty skies
at my com - mand, my love.

3rd time D. C. al coda

CODA

and last___ till the end___ of time, my love. The first time___ ev- er I saw___ your face,_____ your face,___ your face,___ your face,___ your face.____

rall.

FROM BOTH SIDES NOW

Words and Music by JONI MITCHELL

HARRY

Words and Music by CATHERINE HOWE

HE WAS BEAUTIFUL (CAVATINA)

Words by CLEO LAINE
Music by STANLEY MYERS

HELP ME MAKE IT THROUGH THE NIGHT

Words and Music by KRIS KRISTOFFERSON

HOW DEEP IS YOUR LOVE

Words and Music by BARRY, ROBIN and MAURICE GIBB

Fm7 B♭m D♭maj7 Gm Fm

down in - side that I real - ly do. And it's me you need to show.

B♭11 E♭

How deep is your love, is your love? How deep is your love?

A♭maj7 Fm A♭m E♭

I real - ly need to learn. 'Cause we're liv - ing in a world of fools

B♭m/D♭ C7 C7(♭9) C7

break - ing us down, when they all should let us be.

HI HO SILVER LINING

Words and Music by SCOTT ENGLISH and LAURENCE WEISS

I DON'T WANT TO PUT A HOLD ON YOU

Words and Music by MICHAEL and BERNI FLINT

If you wan - na leave— me, well, that's all right.

Come the morn - in'— find you're gone, well, well, I won't mind.

find that you're in__ need of a change, well, well, I won't mind.

Don't mis-un-der-stand__ me, ba-by, my love is true,__

D. %. al coda ⊕

but I don't want to put no hold__ on you.

D. %. al coda ⊕

I'LL GO WHERE YOUR MUSIC TAKES ME

Words and Music by BIDDU

where your mu - sic takes me, ___ where your rhy - thm

makes me, ___ that's where my des - ti - ny

I'll go ___

I'M NOT IN LOVE

Words and Music by ERIC STEWART and GRAHAM GOULDMAN

And just be - cause_____ I call you up,_____ don't get me wrong, don't think you've got it made.__ I'm not in love,___ I'm not__ in love._____

(14 times - fade from the 13th.)

ISN'T SHE LOVELY

Words and Music by STEVIE WONDER

IT'S A HEARTACHE

Words and Music by RONNIE SCOTT and STEVE WOLFE

JAMBALAYA (ON THE BAYOU)

Words and Music by HANK WILLIAMS

3.
Settle down far from town, get me a pirogue
And I'll catch all the fish in the bayou
Swap my mon to buy Yvonne what she need-o
Son of a gun, we'll have big fun on the bayou

JOLENE

Words and Music by DOLLY PARTON

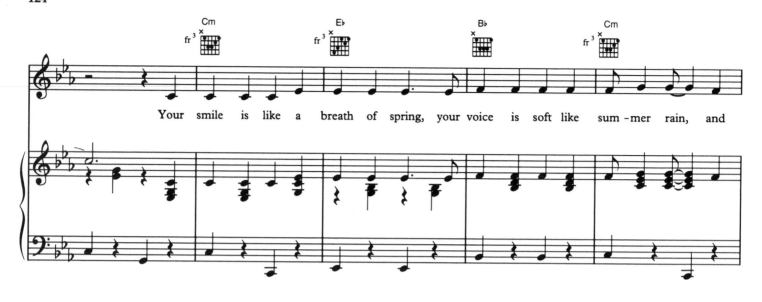

Your smile is like a breath of spring, your voice is soft like sum-mer rain, and

I can-not com-pete with you Jo-lene.＿＿＿ He

talks a - bout you in his sleep and there's no-thing I＿ can do to keep from
You could have＿ your choice of men, but I could ne - ver love a-gain.＿

cry - ing when he calls your name Jo - lene._____
He's the on - ly one for me Jo - lene._____

And I can eas - 'ly un - der - stand__ how you could eas - 'ly
I had to have this talk with you,__ my hap - pi - ness de -

take my man, but you don't know what he means to me Jo - lene._____
pends on you__ and what - ev - er you de - cide to do Jo - lene._____

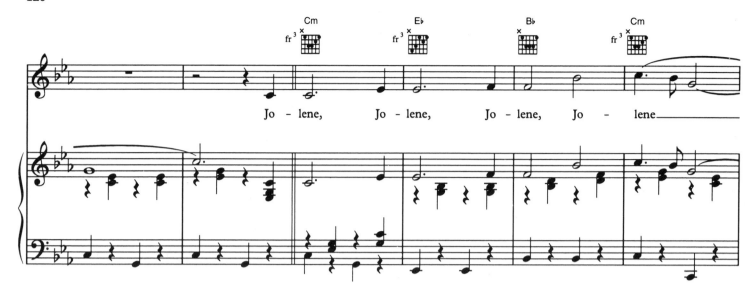

Jo - lene, Jo - lene, Jo - lene, Jo - lene

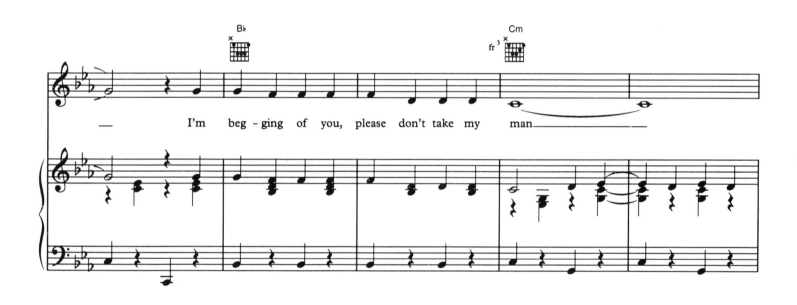

I'm beg-ging of you, please don't take my man

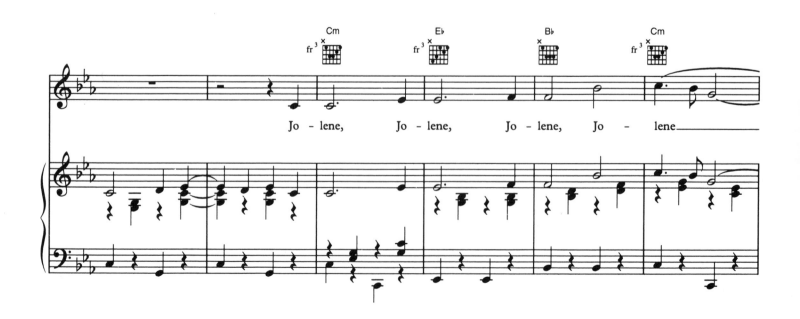

Jo - lene, Jo - lene, Jo - lene, Jo - lene

please don't take him just be- cause you can.
ev - en though you

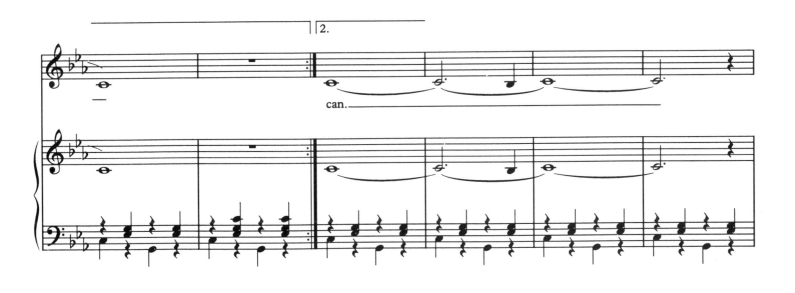

can.

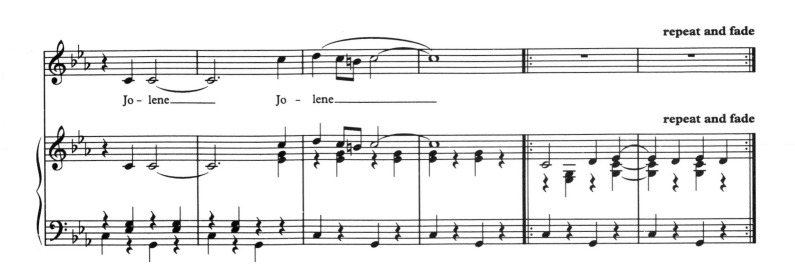

Jo - lene ___ Jo - lene ___

repeat and fade

THE LAST FAREWELL

Words by RONALD ARTHUR WEBSTER
Music by ROGER WHITTAKER

dear - ly than the spo - ken word can tell. For you are

beau - ti - ful, and I have loved you dear - ly, more dear - ly than the spo - ken word can

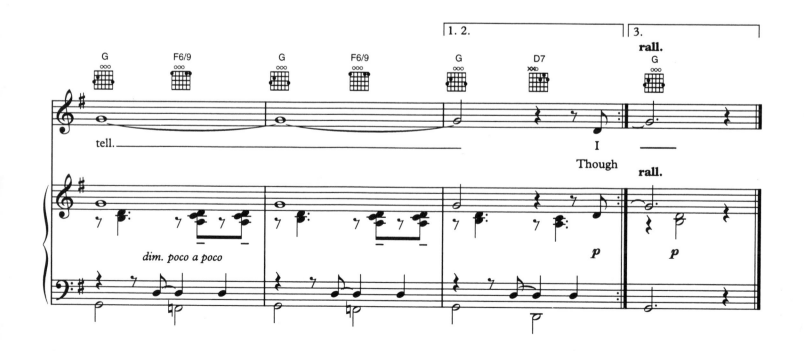

tell.

Though

I

THE LIFE AND TIMES OF DAVID LLOYD GEORGE

By ENNIO MORRICONE

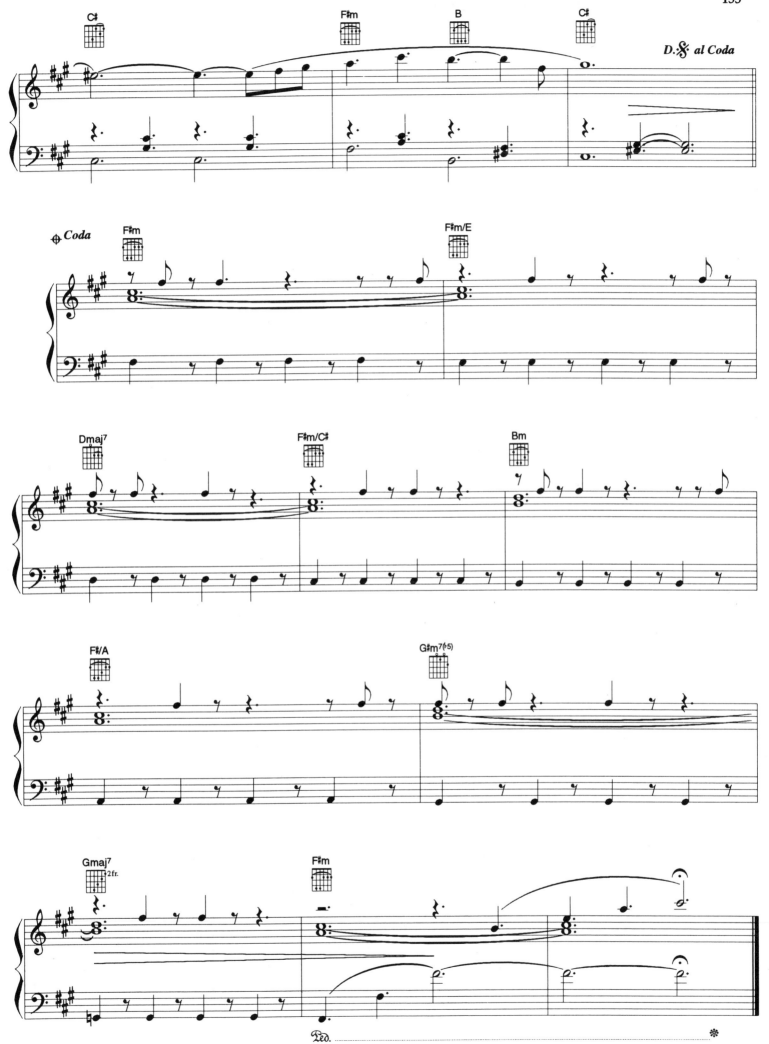

LEAVING ON A JET PLANE

Words and Music by JOHN DENVER

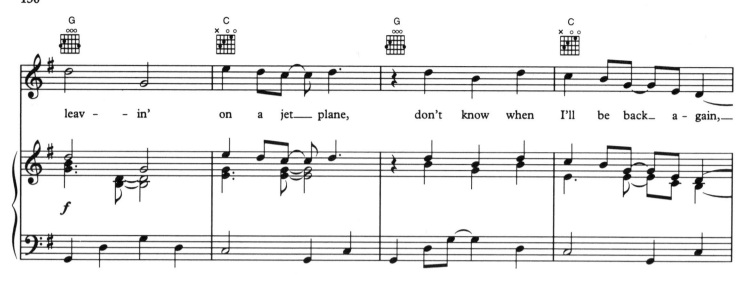

leav - -in' on a jet___ plane, don't know when I'll be back___ a - gain,

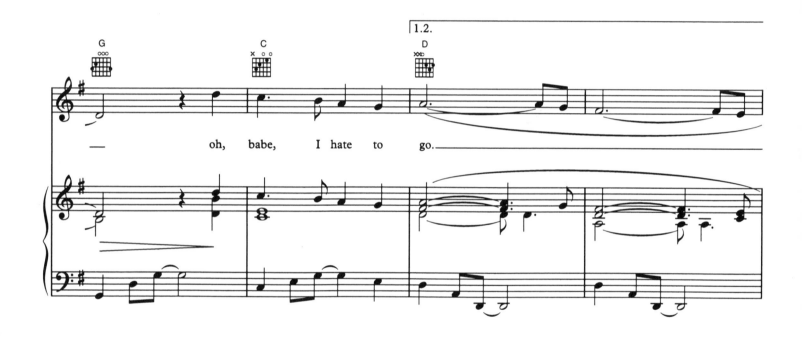

oh, babe, I hate to go.___

(2.) There's so go.___ I'm leav - in'

(3.) ———

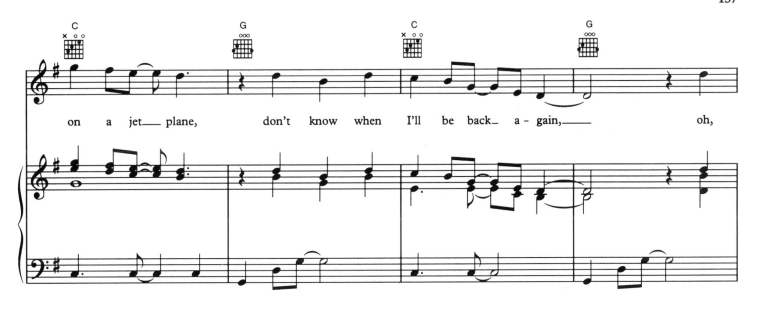

on a jet___ plane, don't know when I'll be back___ a - gain,_____ oh,

babe,_____ I hate to go._____

LOST IN FRANCE

Words and Music by RONNIE SCOTT and STEVE WOLFE

lost in France in the fields the birds were sing - ing. I was
lost in France in the street a band was play - ing, and the
lost in France and the vines were o - ver flow - ing, I was

lost in France, and the day was just be - gin - ning, I just
crowd all danced, did - n't catch what they were say - ing, when I
lost in France, and a mil - lion stars were glow - ing, and I

stood there   in the morn - ing rain,_   I had   a   feel - ing I   can't ex - plain,
looked up   he was stand - ing there,   I knew I should - n't but I   did - n't care,   I was
looked round   for a tel - e - phone to say   ba - by I   won't   be home,

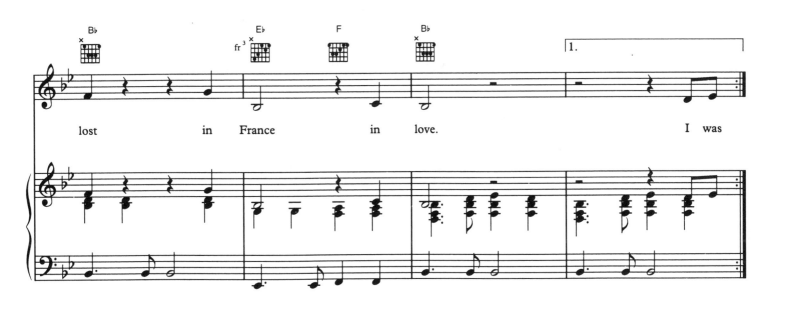

lost   in France   in love.   I was

Oo la   la la oo la___ la la dance,   oo la la la danc - ing,

oo la la la oo la____ la la dance, oo la la la danc - ing,

oo la la la oo la____ la la dance, oo la la la danc - ing,

to coda ⊕   D. 𝄋 al coda

I was

to coda ⊕   D. 𝄋 al coda

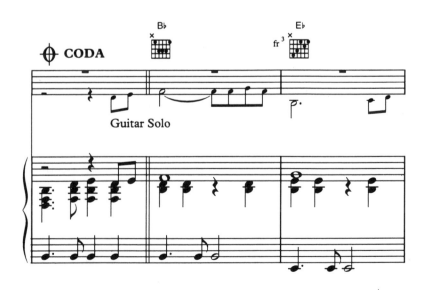

⊕ CODA

Guitar Solo

And I looked round for a tel- e -phone to say ba - by I won't be home, I was lost in France in love.

repeat till fade

Oo la la la oo la la la dance, oo la la la danc - ing,

repeat till fade

LOVE IS LIKE A BUTTERFLY

Words and Music by DOLLY PARTON

MATCHSTALK MEN
AND MATCHSTALK CATS AND DOGS

Words and Music by MICHAEL COLEMAN and BRIAN BURKE

MANDY

Words and Music by RICHARD KERR and SCOTT ENGLISH

I re-mem-ber all my life ___ rain-ing down as cold as ice. ___
morn-ing just an-oth-er day; ___ hap-py peo-ple pass my way. ___
stand-ing on the edge of time; ___ I've walked a-way when love was mine. ___

Shad-ows of a man, a face through a win-dow,
Look-ing in their eyes, I
Caught up in a world of

MORE THAN A WOMAN

Words and Music by BARRY, ROBIN and MAURICE GIBB

MUSIC

Words and Music by JOHN MILES

my mu-sic pulls me through.

(Instrumental Solo)

dim - in - u - en - do poco a poco

A tempo 1°♩ = ♩

Mu - sic was my first love and it will be my

last, mu - sic of the fu - ture and mu - sic of the past,

and mu - sic of the past, and mu - sic of the past.

NEW YORK, NEW YORK

Words by FRED EBB
Music by JOHN KANDER

CODA

king of the hill, head of the list, cream of the crop at the top of the heap.

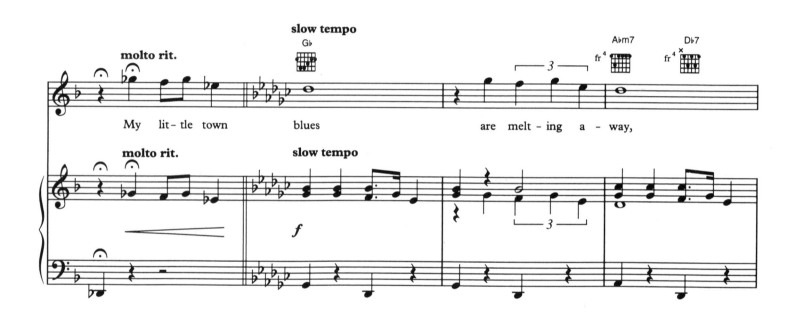

My lit–tle town blues are melt–ing a–way,

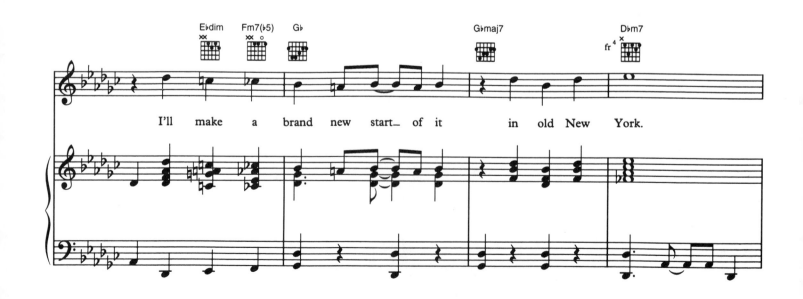

I'll make a brand new start— of it in old New York.

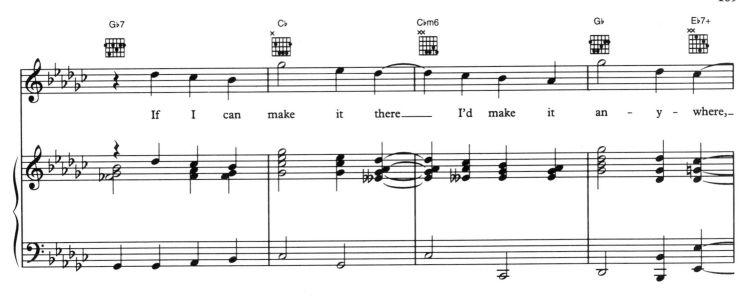

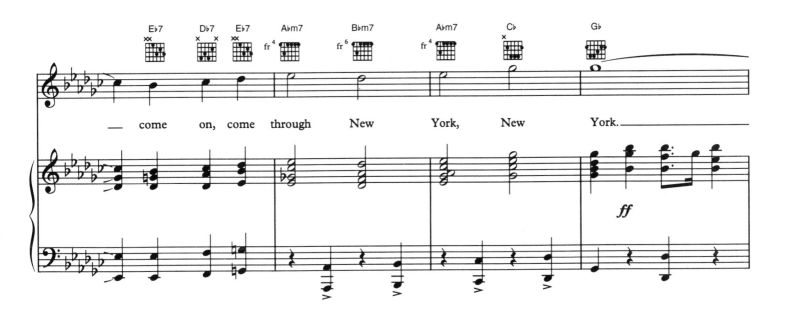

NOBODY DOES IT BETTER

Words by CAROLE BAYER-SAGER
Music by MARVIN HAMLISCH

PALOMA BLANCA

Words and Music by J BOUWENS

I'm just a bird in the sky._____
o - ver the moun-tains I fly.__

No one can take_____ my free-dom a - way._____

Oo_____

Repeat and fade

THE OLD FASHIONED WAY

Original Words by CHARLES AZNAVOUR
English Words by AL KASHA and JOEL HIRSCHHORN
Music by GEORGES GARVARENTZ

RHINESTONE COWBOY

Words and Music by LARRY WEISS

ROCKIN' ALL OVER THE WORLD

Words and Music by JOHN CAMERON FOGERTY

(1.) gid – dy up and gid – dy up and get a – -way, we're go – ing cra – zy and we're

(2.) Instrumental

(3.) gon – na tell your mam – ma what you're gon – na do. Come on a – round___ get your

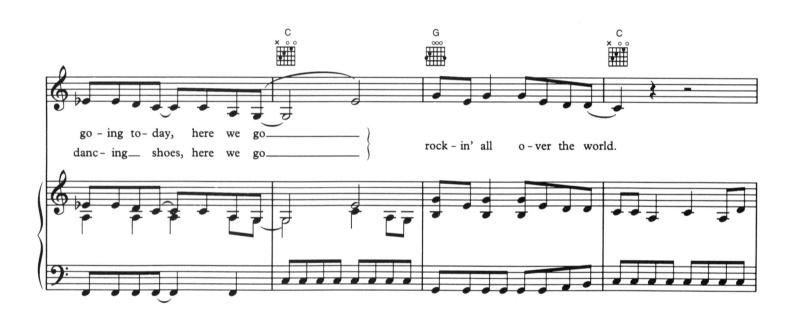

go – ing to-day, here we go_____)
danc – ing___ shoes, here we go_____) rock – in' all o -ver the world.

And I like – it, I like___ it, I like___ it, I like___ it, I la___ la la like___ it, la___

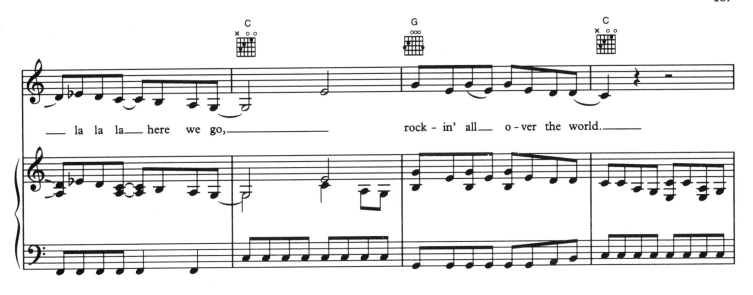

la la la here we go, _____ rock-in' all__ o-ver the world.____

1.   2.   3.

I'm   And I like__ it, I like_ it, I like

__ it, I like_ it, I la__ la la like_ it, la__ la la la, here we go,__

rock - in' all___ o - ver the world.___

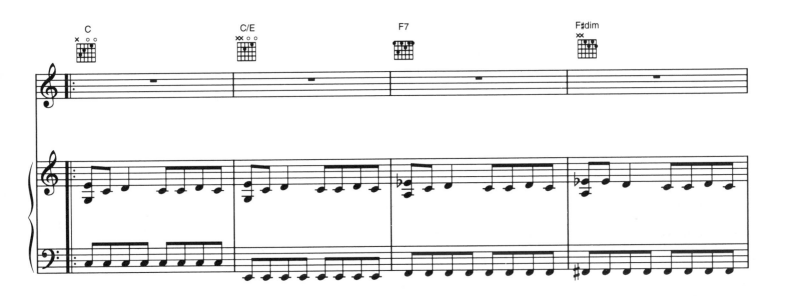

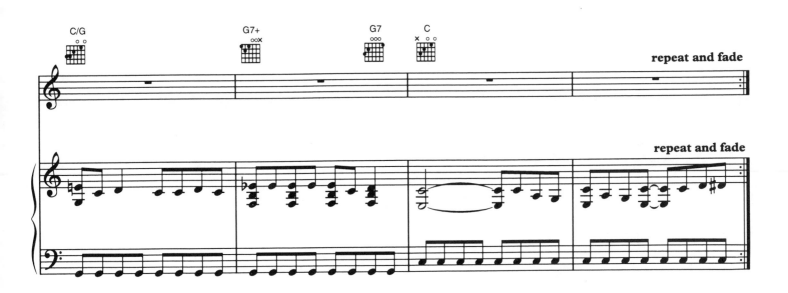

repeat and fade

repeat and fade

SAVE YOUR KISSES FOR ME

Words and Music by TONY HILLER, MARTIN LEE & LEE SHERIDAN

ev-'ry-thing I do.__ Now the time is mov-in' on,__ and I real-ly should be gone but you keep
got to work each day__ and that's why I go a-way, but I count

__ me hang-in' on__ for one__ more smile. I love you (I love you) all the while.
__ the se-conds till__ I'm home with you. I love you (I love you) it's

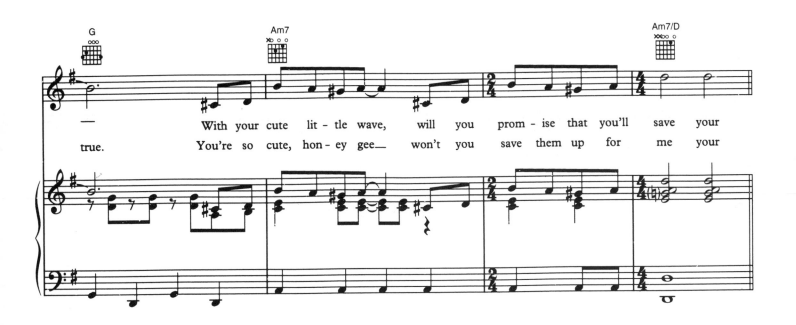

— With your cute lit-tle wave, will you prom-ise that you'll save your
true. You're so cute, hon-ey gee__ won't you save them up for me your

SEND IN THE CLOWNS

Words and Music by STEPHEN SONDHEIM

SING

Words and Music by JOE RAPOSO

Sing! Sing a song. Make it sim-ple to

last your whole life long._____ Don't wor-ry that it's not good e-nough for

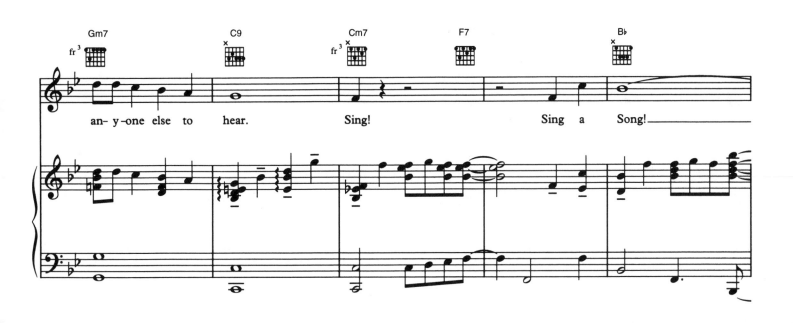

an-y-one else to hear. Sing! Sing a Song!_____

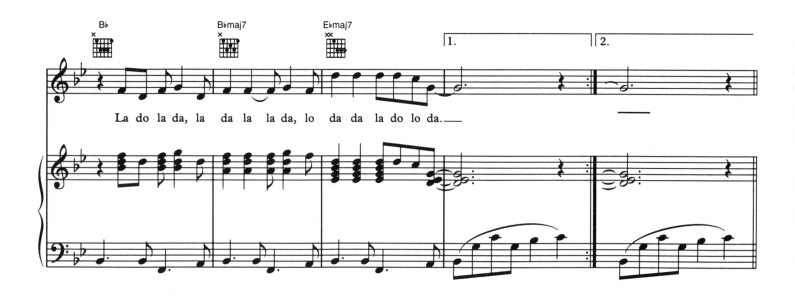

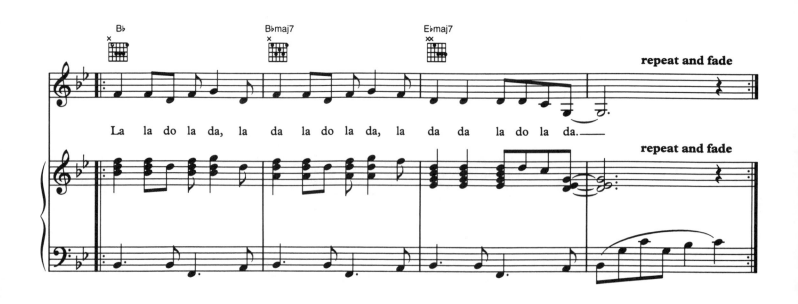

SNOWBIRD

Words and Music by GENE MacLELLAN

one I love__ for-ev-er is un-true_____ and

if I could, you know that I would fly a-way with you._____ The

you._____ Yeah____ if I could, you know that I would

fly_____ a-way with you._____

SOLITAIRE

Words and Music by NEIL SEDAKA and PHIL CODY

pre ——— tend__ he'll nev – er love a ——— gain._____ And

keep – ing to him – self he plays the game._____ With – out her love it al –ways ends the

same._____ While life goes on a – round him ev –'ry – where,_____ he's play – ing

sol - i - taire._____ _____ And sol - i -taire's the on-ly game in

town,_____ and ev-'ry road that takes him, takes him down.____ While life goes on a - round him ev-'ry-

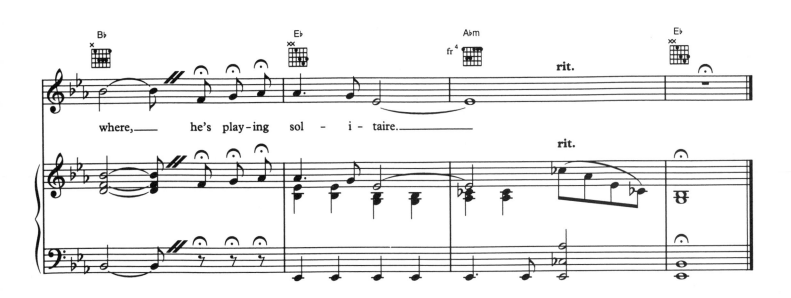

where,____ he's play-ing sol - i - taire._____

STAND BY YOUR MAN

Words and Music by TAMMY WYNETTE and BILLY SHERRILL

STREETS OF LONDON

Words and Music by RALPH McTELL

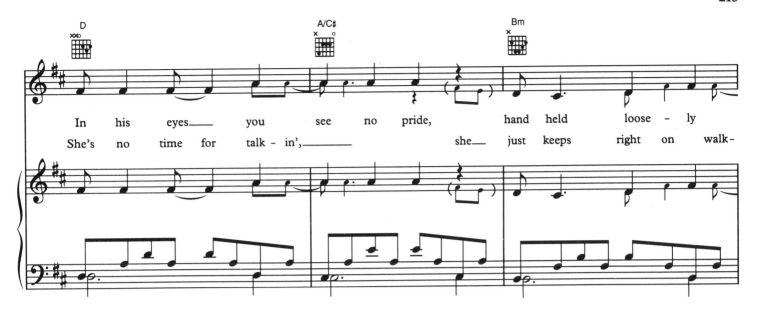

In his eyes___ you see no pride, hand held loose-ly
She's no time for talk-in',_____ she__ just keeps right on walk-

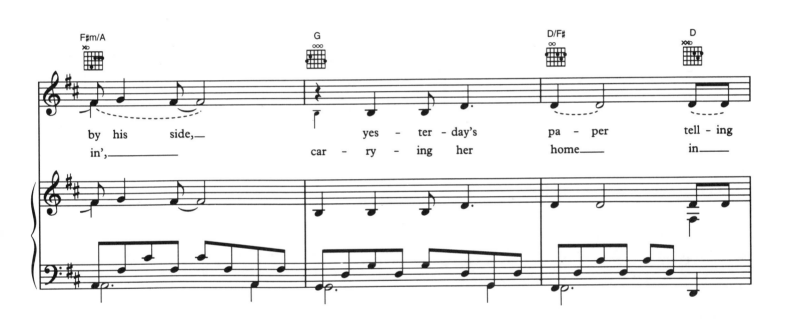

by his side,___ yes - ter-day's pa - per tell - ing
in',_____ car - ry - ing her home___ in___

yes - - ter-day's news._____ So
two car - ri - er bags._____

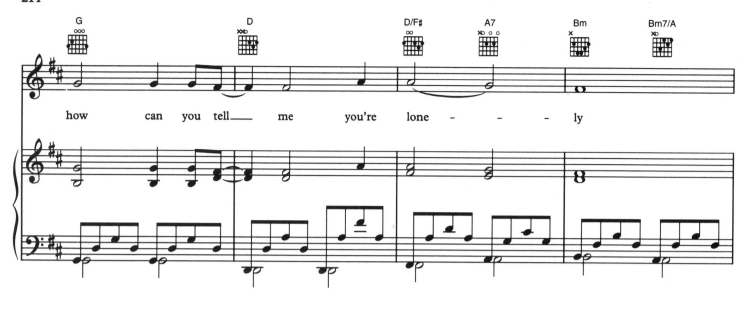

how can you tell___ me you're lone - - - ly

and say for you___ that the sun don't shine?_____

Let me take___ you by the hand and lead you through the streets of Lon - don.

I'll show you some - thing_____ to make you change your

mind.

mind.

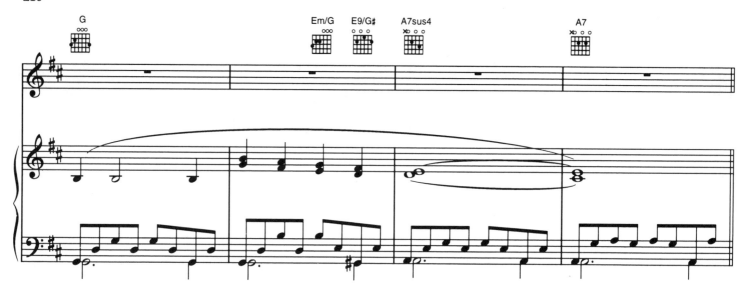

In the all - - night ca - fé at a quart - er past___ e -
Have you seen___ the old man out - side the sea - -man's

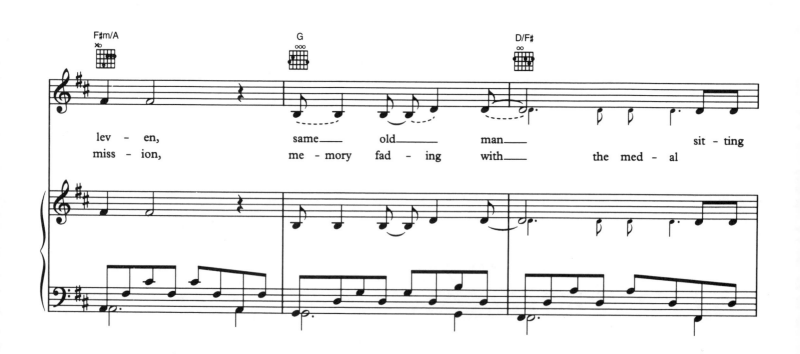

lev - en, same___ old___ man___ sit - ting
miss - ion, me - mory fad - ing with___ the med - al

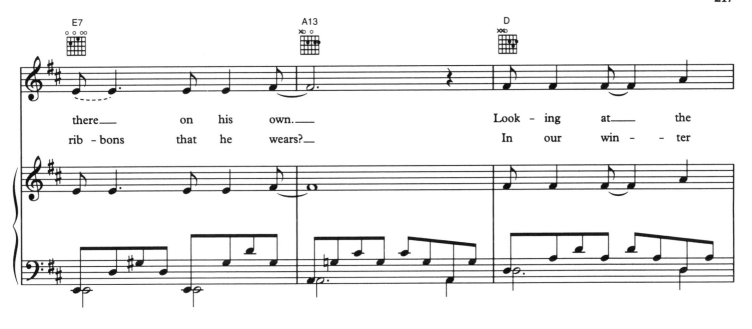

there___ on his own.___   Look - ing at___ the
rib - bons that he wears?___   In our win - - ter

world___ o - ver the rim of his tea - cup.___
ci - ty the rain cries a lit - tle pi - ty___ for one

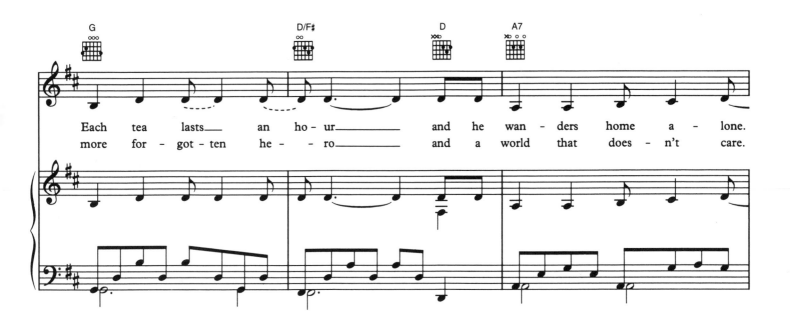

Each tea lasts___ an ho - ur___ and he wan - ders home a - lone.
more for - got - ten he - - ro___ and a world that does - n't care.

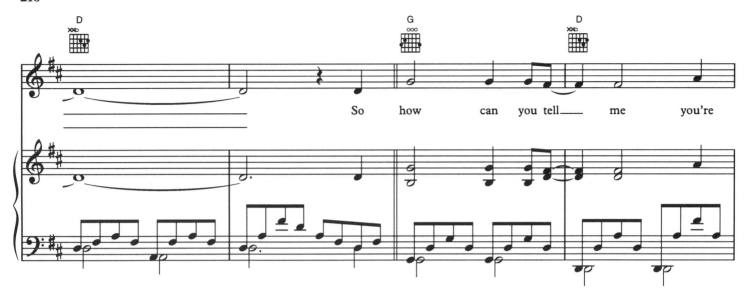

So how can you tell___ me you're

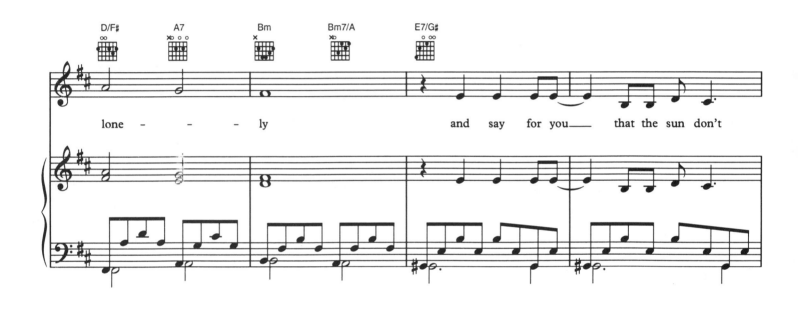

lone - - - ly and say for you___ that the sun don't

shine?___ Let me take___ you by the hand and

TAKE GOOD CARE OF MY BABY

Words and Music by GERRY GOFFIN and CAROLE KING

THREE TIMES A LADY

Words and Music by LIONEL RICHIE

you.

2. You've
3. When

You're

Coda Yes, you're once,___ twice,___

(When) we are together
The moments I cherish
With ev'ry beat of my heart
To touch you, to hold you
To feel you, to need you
There's nothing to keep us apart

TIE A YELLOW RIBBON 'ROUND THE OLE OAK TREE

Words and Music by IRWIN LEVINE and L RUSSELL BROWN

I'm com - ing home___ I've done my time,___
Bus dri - ver please___ look for me___

now I've got to know___ what is___ and is - n't mine.
cause I could - n't bear___ to see___ what I might see.

I don't see a yel - low rib - bon 'round the ole_____ oak
hun - dred yel - low rib - bons 'round the ole ole_____ oak

1. tree._____

2. tree._____

Now the

TOMORROW

Words by MARTIN CHARNIN
Music by CHARLES STROUSE

(small notes are optional harmony)

TOUCH ME IN THE MORNING

Words and Music by RONALD MILLER and MICHAEL MASSER

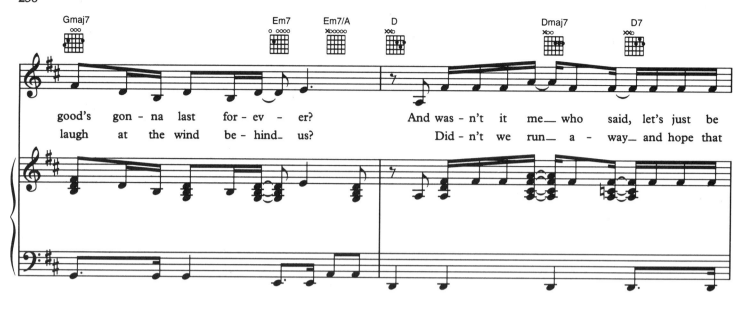

good's gon - na last for - ev - er? And was - n't it me— who said, let's just be
laugh at the wind be - hind— us? Did - n't we run a - way— and hope that

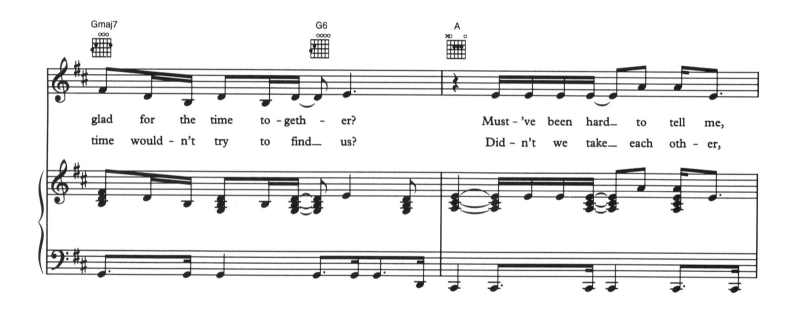

glad for the time to-geth - er? Must - 've been hard— to tell me,
time would - n't try to find— us? Did - n't we take— each oth - er,

that you've giv - en all— you had— to give. I can un - der- stand you feel - in' that way.
to a place where no - one's ev - er been? Yeah I real - ly need you near me to -night.

THE WAY WE WERE

Words by ALAN and MARILYN BERGMAN
Music by MARVIN HAMLISCH

WHAT HAVE THEY DONE TO MY SONG, MA

Words and Music by MELANIE SAFKA

5. Maybe it'll all be alright Ma, maybe it'll all be O.K.
   Well, if the people are buying tears I'll be rich someday, Ma,
   Look what they've done to my song.

7. Look what they've done to my song Ma,
   Look what they've done to my song Ma,
   Well they tied it up in a plastic bag,
   turned it upside down, Ma,
   Look what they've done to my song.

6. Ils ont changé ma chanson, Ma, ils ont changé ma chanson,
   C'est la seule chose que je peux faire et ce n'est pas bon ma,
   Ils ont changé ma chanson.

8. Look what they've done to my song , Ma,
   Look what they've done to my song,
   Well it's the only thing that I could do half right,
   and it's turning out all wrong, Ma
   Look what they've done to my song.

WHEN A CHILD IS BORN

Words by FRED JAY
Music by ZACAR and DARIO BALDAN BEMBO

WHEN I NEED YOU

Words by CAROLE BAYER SAGER
Music by ALBERT HAMMOND

When I need you, _____ I just close my eyes and I'm with

When I need love, I hold out my hands___ and I

touch love. I nev - er knew there was so much

WHEN YOU SMILE

Words and Music by WILLIAM SALTER and RALPH MacDONALD

do or___ die.___
what I___ mean.___
when you___ smile.___

Oh, ba - by let me___ hold
I'm gon - na rock it___ to___
Oh, ba - by let me___ love

___ you.___
___ you.___
___ you.___

You make me want to hold___ you.
I'm gon - na rock it to___ you.
You got - ta let me love___ you.

(1. & 3.) When you___ smile,_____ smile,_____ smile,_____ smile,_____ smile,
(2.) Ev - 'ry___ time,_____ time,_____ time,_____ time,_____ time,

la la la la la_____ la___ la,___ la la la la la la___

__ la. La la__ la,_____ la,_____ la,___

D. %· repeat and fade

_____ la,_____ la,_____ la,_____ la. When you

D. %· repeat and fade

WHERE IS THE LOVE

Words and Music by WILLIAM SALTER and RALPH MacDONALD

Where is the love;— where is the love;— where is the love;

— where is the love; —

Where is the love———— you said you'd
Where is the love———— you said was

give to me,— soon as you were free, will it ev-er be,—
mine, all mine,— till the end of time, was it just a lie,————

where is the love._____
where is the love._____

You told me that you did-n't love him; and you were gon-na say good-
If you had had a sud-den change of heart, I wish that you would tell me
Oh, how I wish I'd nev-er met you, I guess it must have been my

bye;_____ but if you real-ly did-n't mean it,_____
so;_____ don't leave me hang-ing on to prom-is-es,_____
fate_____ to fall in love with some-one else's love,_____

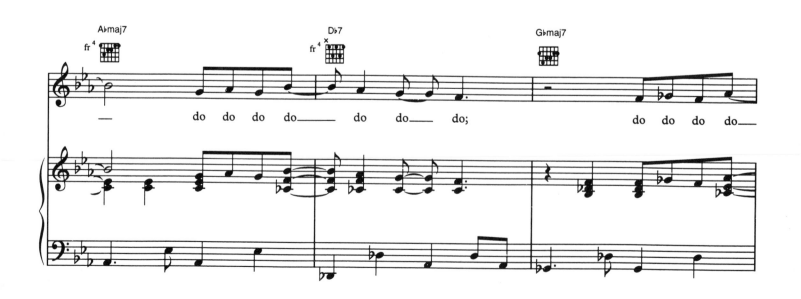

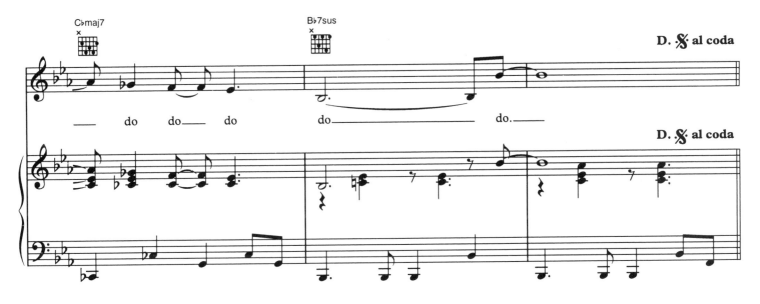

D. %: al coda

do   do   do   do_____   do.____

CODA

_____   That's all I____ can do   yeah,__ yeah,   yeah.

repeat and fade

Where is the love;____   where is the love;_____   where is the love;____   where is the love.

WOMAN IN LOVE

Words and Music by DOMINIC BUGATTI and FRANK MUSKER

It's the same old sto-ry,— you care but you don't love me. Though I knew it, it still hurts to hear the

truth. Don't ex-pect me to for-get you, I love you and I can't hold back the

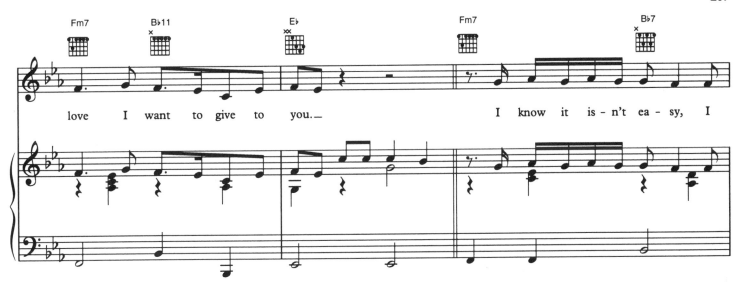

love I want to give to you.___ I know it is-n't ea-sy, I

un-der-stand you feel-ings, and I'm hap-py___ just to see you___ when I can._____ Do you

un-der-stand my rea-sons? I love you and a wo-man in love___ loves on-ly one man.

Just give me love when you can___ if you need me.___ A wo-man in love

will un-der-stand.___ And I'll give you all that I am___ com-

plete-ly.___ A wo-man in love___ loves on-ly one man.___

So don't be sor - ry, ba - by,___ I guess you think I'm cra - zy but to

be there when you want me___ is e - nough._____ I'm not a child,_ I'm a wo -man, I

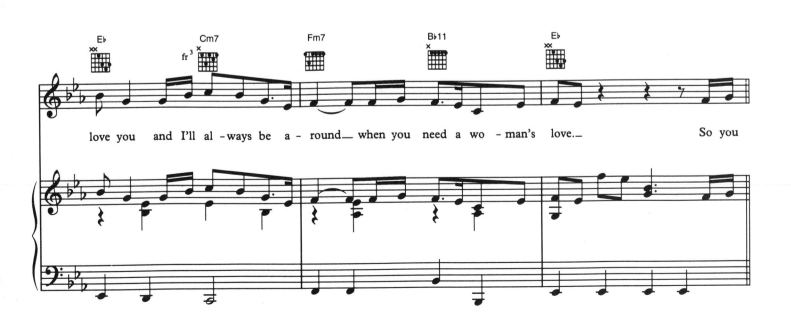

love you and I'll al -ways be a - round___ when you need a wo -man's love.___ So you

see it's the same old sto-ry, you care but you don't love me. Though I

knew it,___ it still hurts to hear the truth._____ I'm no child,_ I'm a wo-man. I

D. %. and fade

love you and I'll al-ways be a-round_ when you need a wo-man's love.___ Just give me

D. %. and fade

WUTHERING HEIGHTS

Words and Music by KATE BUSH

YOU ARE THE SUNSHINE OF MY LIFE

Words and Music by STEVIE WONDER

Though I've loved you___ for a mil - lion years,___
Be - cause you came___ to my___ res - cue,___

and if I thought our love___ was end - ing,___
and I know that___ this must___ be heav - en,___

I'd find___ my - self___ drown - ing in my___ own___
how could so much love be___ in - side___ of

tears.   Whoa_____ whoa_____ you?   Whoa_____

_____ You are the sun - shine of__ my life.__
You are the ap - ple of__ my eye.__

(fade 3rd time)

That's why I'll al - ways be__ a - round._____
For - ev - er__ you'll__ stay in__ my heart._____

(fade 3rd time)

YOU DON'T BRING ME FLOWERS

Words by NEIL DIAMOND
Music by NEIL DIAMOND, MARILYN BERGMAN and ALAN BERGMAN

YOU LIGHT UP MY LIFE

Words and Music by JOE BROOKS

CODA

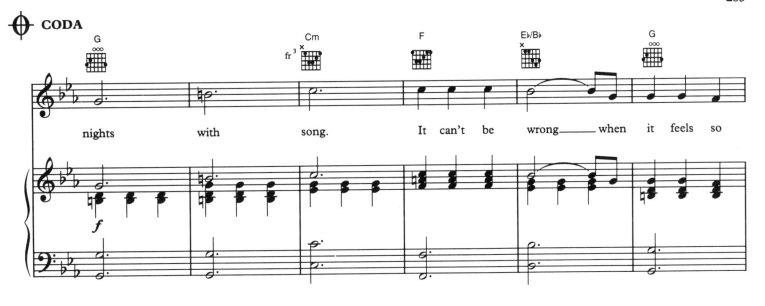

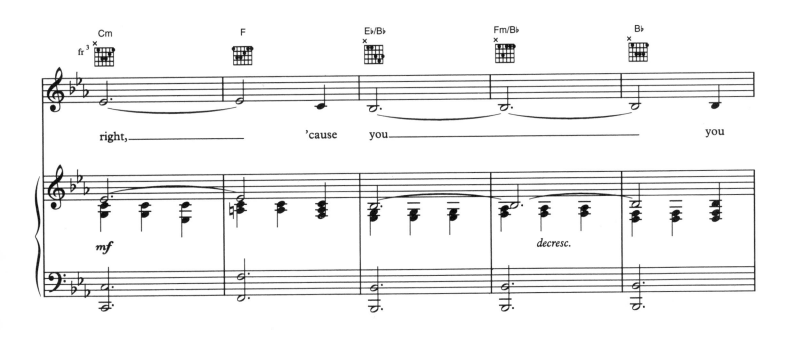

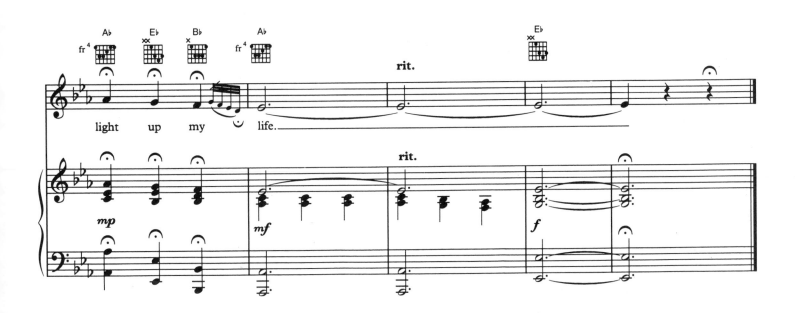

YOU NEEDED ME

Words and Music by CHARLES R GOODRUM

YOU'RE A LADY

Words and Music by PETER SKELLERN

Now the ev'-ning has come to a close and I've had my last dance with
Hard to ans-wer, yes, I a-gree — but then I've got to

you. On to the emp-ty streets we go
know; I'm not ask-ing you to mar-ry me —

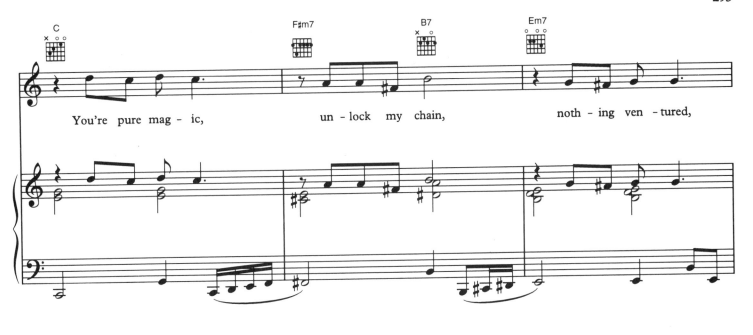

You're pure mag - ic,   un - lock my chain,   noth - ing ven -tured,

noth - ing gained.   And so I say with   no re -straint, "Be

mine,   be mine."   mine."

YOU'VE GOT A FRIEND

Words and Music by CAROLE KING

When you're down

and trou - bled and you need some love and care and
a - bove you grows dark and full of clouds and

noth - in', noth - in' is go - in' right, and
that ol' north wind be - gins to blow, and

close your eyes and think of me and soon I will be there to
keep your head to - geth - er and call my name out loud; to

100 YEARS OF POPULAR MUSIC

International MUSIC Publications

IMP's Exciting New Series!

100 YEARS OF POPULAR MUSIC

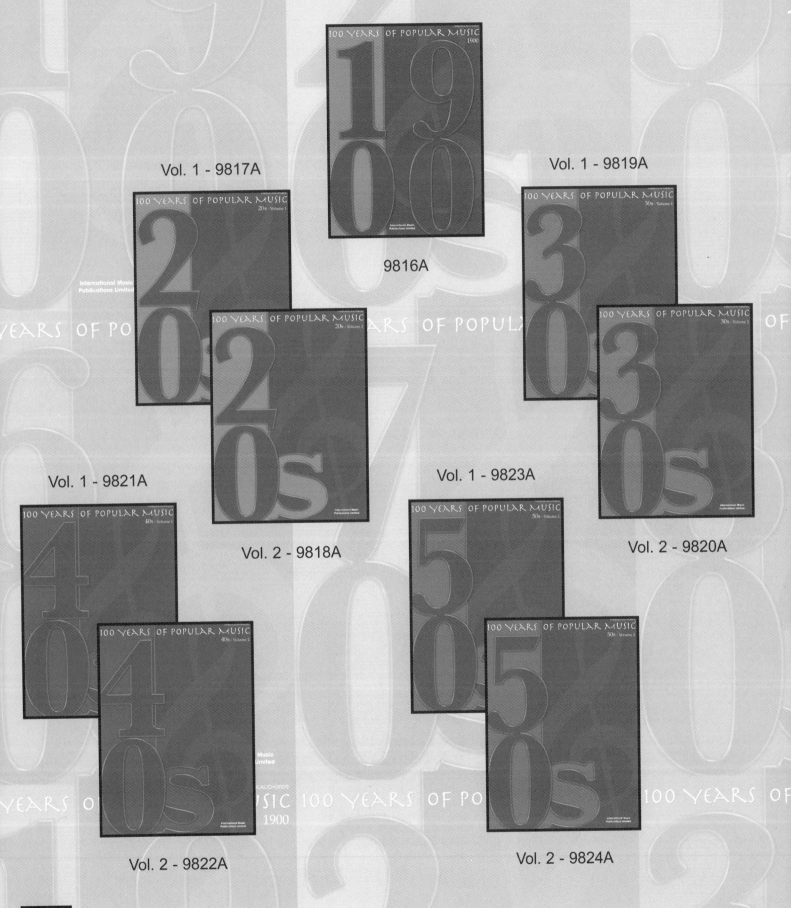

Vol. 1 - 9817A

9816A

Vol. 1 - 9819A

Vol. 1 - 9821A

Vol. 2 - 9818A

Vol. 1 - 9823A

Vol. 2 - 9820A

Vol. 2 - 9822A

Vol. 2 - 9824A

International
MUSIC
Publications

IMP's Exciting New Series!

100 YEARS OF POPULAR MUSIC

Vol. 1 - 9825A

Vol. 1 - 9827A

Vol. 1 - 9829A

Vol. 1 - 9831A

Vol. 2 - 9826A

Vol. 2 - 9828A

Vol. 2 - 9830A

Vol. 2 - 9832A

Vol. 2 - 9833A

International
MUSIC
Publications

IMP's Exciting New Series!